Flyovers

by Jeffrey Sweet

A Samuel French Acting Edition

Copyright © 2006, 2010 by Jeffrey Sweet

ALL RIGHTS RESERVED

CAUTION: Professionals and amateurs are hereby warned that *FLYOVERS* is subject to a Licensing Fee. It is fully protected under the copyright laws of the United States of America, the British Commonwealth, including Canada, and all other countries of the Copyright Union. All rights, including professional, amateur, motion picture, recitation, lecturing, public reading, radio broadcasting, television and the rights of translation into foreign languages are strictly reserved. In its present form the play is dedicated to the reading public only.

The amateur live stage performance rights to *FLYOVERS* are controlled exclusively by Samuel French, Inc., and licensing arrangements and performance licenses must be secured well in advance of presentation. PLEASE NOTE that amateur Licensing Fees are set upon application in accordance with your producing circumstances. When applying for a licensing quotation and a performance license please give us the number of performances intended, dates of production, your seating capacity and admission fee. Licensing Fees are payable one week before the opening performance of the play to Samuel French, Inc., at 45 W. 25th Street, New York, NY 10010.

Licensing Fee of the required amount must be paid whether the play is presented for charity or gain and whether or not admission is charged.

Stock licensing fees quoted upon application to Samuel French, Inc.

For all other rights than those stipulated above, apply to: Abrams Artists Agency, 275 Seventh Avenue, 26th Floor, New York, NY 10001 Attn: Morgan Jenness.

Particular emphasis is laid on the question of amateur or professional readings, permission and terms for which must be secured in writing from Samuel French, Inc.

Copying from this book in whole or in part is strictly forbidden by law, and the right of performance is not transferable.

Whenever the play is produced the following notice must appear on all programs, printing and advertising for the play: "Produced by special arrangement with Samuel French, Inc."

Due authorship credit must be given on all programs, printing and advertising for the play.

ISBN 978-0-573-69870-5   Printed in U.S.A.   #29528

No one shall commit or authorize any act or omission by which the copyright of, or the right to copyright, this play may be impaired.

No one shall make any changes in this play for the purpose of production.

Publication of this play does not imply availability for performance. Both amateurs and professionals considering a production are strongly advised in their own interests to apply to Samuel French, Inc., for written permission before starting rehearsals, advertising, or booking a theatre.

No part of this book may be reproduced, stored in a retrieval system, or transmitted in any form, by any means, now known or yet to be invented, including mechanical, electronic, photocopying, recording, videotaping, or otherwise, without the prior written permission of the publisher.

MUSIC USE NOTE

Licensees are solely responsible for obtaining formal written permission from copyright owners to use copyrighted music in the performance of this play and are strongly cautioned to do so. If no such permission is obtained by the licensee, then the licensee must use only original music that the licensee owns and controls. Licensees are solely responsible and liable for all music clearances and shall indemnify the copyright owners of the play and their licensing agent, Samuel French, Inc., against any costs, expenses, losses and liabilities arising from the use of music by licensees.

IMPORTANT BILLING AND CREDIT REQUIREMENTS

All producers of *FLYOVERS* must give credit to the Author of the Play in all programs distributed in connection with performances of the Play, and in all instances in which the title of the Play appears for the purposes of advertising, publicizing or otherwise exploiting the Play and/or a production. The name of the Author *must* appear on a separate line on which no other name appears, immediately following the title and *must* appear in size of type not less than fifty percent of the size of the title type.

In addition the following credit *must* be given in all programs and publicity information distributed in association with this piece:

> **FLYOVERS was developed through a series of private readings and explorations.**
> **FLYOVERS received its premiere at the**
> **Victory Gardens Theatre of Chicago on May 21, 1998.**
> **FLYOVERS received its New York premiere at the**
> **78th Street Theatre on February 1, 2009.**

FLYOVERS received its premiere at the Victory Gardens Theatre of Chicago on May 21, 1998. The production was directed by Dennis Zacek, the theatre's artistic director. The cast was as follows:

TED	William Petersen
OLIVER	Marc Vann
IRIS	Amy Morton
LIANNE	Linda Reiter

FLYOVERS received its New York premiere at the 78th Street Theatre on February 1, 2009. The producers were Artistic New Directions (Kristine Niven and Janice Goldberg, artistic co-directors), 78th St. Theater Lab, and Jeff Landsman. It was directed by Sandy Shinner. The cast was as follows:

TED	Kevin Geer
OLIVER	Richard Kind
IRIS	Michele Pawk
LIANNE	Donna Bullock

CHARACTERS

Ted
Oliver
Iris
Lianne

To Lindsay Crouse

Scene One

(The time is 1998. The deck of **TED**'s *house in a housing development in downstate Ohio. A barbeque, outdoor bar, etc.* **TED** *is making a drink for* **OLIVER**. **OLIVER** *wears a jacket and tie. They and all of the characters in the play are in their forties. The scene begins at twilight and continues into the evening.)*

TED. You really get into it sometimes, the two of you. You and, uh –

OLIVER. Sarah.

TED. Sarah, yeah. Sometimes you seem to be really –

OLIVER. Well, that's part of the fun of it.

TED. – really pissed at each other.

OLIVER. No, not pissed.

TED. She doesn't tick you off? Her attitude: "Of course you'd like that piece of crap, Oliver, it's got explosions and butts and boobs. Cuz you're a guy." That doesn't make you –

OLIVER. That's part of the act.

TED. The act? You mean it's a phony?

OLIVER. No, the opinions we have are the opinions we have. But the idea of the show – the thing that makes our show different from Siskel and Ebert or those other guys – is that it's a man and a woman. The idea – the way we sold it to the syndicator – was a lot of couples go to the movies together –

TED. I think they call those "dates."

OLIVER. – and they end up talking about the same kind of stuff, *issues*, we get into on –

TED. So you're, what? – representing these couples?

OLIVER. Sort of.

TED. She's talking about the movie from, like, the woman's point-of-view, and you're doing it from the guy's?

OLIVER. More or less.

TED. So you're supposed to be the male point-of-view. What? Representing?

OLIVER. Pretty much.

TED. Representing, for instance, me?

OLIVER. You?

TED. I'm a male. I have a male point-of-view.

OLIVER. You put it that way –

TED. Hunh. You like movies with subtitles, right?

OLIVER. I like some of them.

TED. I like none of them. So right there, you don't represent me. You don't speak for *my* male point-of-view.

OLIVER. I don't have your confidence.

TED. Not when it comes to movies.

OLIVER. Well, no two people are going to have the same taste, the same perspective.

TED. But my bet is that you and that woman –

OLIVER. Sarah.

TED. – yeah, see more eye-to-eye about movies than you and me would. That the two of you would probably agree with each other more often about what is or isn't a shitty movie than you and me. This, despite the fact that you and me, we're both guys, which is something you and she don't have in common.

OLIVER. Your point?

TED. I think I just said it.

OLIVER. I guess I missed –

TED. You and her – a man and a woman – have more in common than you and me, who are two guys. But you'd normally think it would be the two guys who have more in common.

OLIVER. That's the point you're making?

TED. Yes. That's my point.

OLIVER. Fair enough.

(**TED** *refills* **OLIVER***'s glass.*)

TED. You ever get it on?

OLIVER. Get it on?

TED. You and Sarah.

OLIVER. No.

TED. People ask you that a lot, don't they?

OLIVER. Anytime people see a man and a woman together, they think there's that possibility.

TED. They think it's a possibility because there *is* that possibility. Any man, any woman, the possibility exists. As long as your equipment is functioning. Unless there's been some horrible accident that makes it impossible –

OLIVER. No, but thank you for your concern.

TED. But the idea has occurred.

OLIVER. What?

TED. You and her.

OLIVER. I'm married.

TED. And that proves what? You like movies with subtitles so much. Anytime somebody in one of those movies is married, you *know* they're gonna be jumping on someone else. That they're married is the tip-off. They're married *so that* they can cheat.

OLIVER. Hey, I just *review* movies. I don't live them.

TED. So you and her – never?

OLIVER. Well, if we did, Ted, you'd be the first person I'd tell.

TED. Right.

OLIVER. Would fifty bucks be useful?

TED. For what?

OLIVER. You were talking before about a plaque. For Mr. Kelly when he retires.

TED. That's generous.

OLIVER. Well, what the hell, he was always nice to me. So, what do you figure for the inscription?

TED. Inscription?

OLIVER. On the plaque. Something about the occasion or the purpose or whatever.

TED. *You're* the writer – what do you think?

OLIVER. OK – "To Mr. Kelly in acknowledgment of, uh, recognition of…uh with *thanks* for – " When did he start teaching? What year?

TED. 1962.

OLIVER. So, 1962 from 1998 is –

TED. Thirty-six.

OLIVER. Thirty-six?

TED. Ninety-eight minus sixty-two –

OLIVER. " – thirty-six years of inspiration as a teacher and a friend." Something like that. Maybe an engraving of a test tube or a Bunsen burner.

TED. Sure, that ought to bring a tear to his eye. That chair of yours looks wobbly.

OLIVER. I'm sorry?

TED. The chair you're on. Something wrong with the leg.

OLIVER. Seems OK –

TED. No, no, move back and forth. Come on.

*(**OLIVER** hesitates, then does it.)*

I thought so.

*(**TED** heads up to the door to the kitchen.)*

Last thing I need is the chair collapses under you, you break your ass and your insurance company comes after –

OLIVER. Where are you –

TED. Just gonna get –

*(He disappears into the house. **OLIVER** remains sitting for a second. Then he moves back and forth on the chair to test the leg. A beat. He stands up and moves over to lean against the railing. **TED** returns with a screwdriver.)*

TED. *(cont.)* This'll just be a second.

(He turns over the chair.)

Just what I thought – the screw's nearly out.

(He begins to work on the chair.)

If we *really* wanted to thank him for years of being a teacher and a friend – Kelly – we'd help him escape this place.

OLIVER. Escape?

TED. This town.

OLIVER. What's wrong with it?

TED. Nothing, if you like corpses.

OLIVER. I don't know.

TED. No, you don't.

OLIVER. No, I didn't mean – I didn't say "I don't know" as in "I don't have a clue."

TED. No? How then?

OLIVER. More in the spirit of, "I'm not sure if I agree with you." With what you said. The opinion you –

TED. It's not an opinion. This town – if we had any decency, any feeling for what this place means or used to mean – to some of us, anyway – we'd haul in a huge fucking pile of dirt – a mountain – and just dump it on top, maybe put up a cross. Honor its memory, sure. Visit once in a while with flowers, but let it just be what it is, which is –

OLIVER. Dead?

*(**TED** finishes futzing with the chair, turns it over, offers it to **OLIVER**.)*

TED. There.

OLIVER. *(sitting)* Yes, I can tell the difference.

TED. Why don't you take off your jacket? Get comfortable.

OLIVER. Why not.

*(During the following, **OLIVER** takes off his jacket and drapes it over the chair. He takes off the tie, too.)*

TED. Do you get paid extra if they put your name in the ads?

OLIVER. Paid?

TED. Something I was wondering. I see your name in the ads. Quotes from you. "Bruce Willis's best since *Hudson Hawk*!"

OLIVER. I didn't say that.

TED. "A film to touch the heart and stir the soul."

OLIVER. I might have said that. About something. Not *Hudson Hawk*. But no, they don't pay me.

TED. That doesn't seem right. They're your words. They use them. Your words put butts on the seats in the theater. Your words help them make money. No, I think they ought to pay you.

OLIVER. But then there would be doubt –

TED. How?

OLIVER. – about whether I really like the movie.

TED. Well, they'd only pay you if you really did.

OLIVER. But how would they know that?

TED. Because you said, "I really like this movie."

OLIVER. Yes, but how would they know that I said so because I really did, or because I'd like to pick up some change so I said I liked something I didn't like?

TED. Because you wouldn't do that.

OLIVER. Yes, but people know I wouldn't do that because there isn't any *reason* for them to suspect my integrity.

TED. OK. I see what you're getting at.

OLIVER. The whole point of credibility as a critic is that you have the reputation of someone whose opinion you can trust. Not that you necessarily agree with it, but that at least –

TED. – they think you're honest.

OLIVER. Yes.

TED. That's important – honesty. What you said, integrity.

OLIVER. Well, it's important in general, of course –

TED. Sure.

OLIVER. – but in what I do –

TED. Sure. I see that.

(a beat)

You'd probably be glad, right? If this place gave up the ghost.

OLIVER. Glad?

TED. This town. What does it mean to you, anyway? Memories? Not ones you want to remember, I bet. We made your life hell here. And we intended to.

OLIVER. Oh, I'm sure –

TED. No, we didn't like you. "We?" OK, "I." Though I wasn't alone. First time I saw you, I think it was in Miss Kingman's class, first time I saw you – the pens in your pocket, the glasses – I didn't know your name, I didn't know if you were Jewish or Greek or Albanian. But you carried your books like a girl – well, you *did* – and you had a crease in your slacks –

OLIVER. So my fate was sealed.

TED. Dead meat on sight. First time I see you, I can already picture you trying not to cry and crying anyway. And the next day you coming to school with some kind of tape wrapped around the middle of your glasses to hold them together where I snapped them in two. I was a mean little bastard. And don't you say, you "don't know," because that's something you *do* know. You of all people. I was an asshole. I beat you without pity.

OLIVER. OK, accepted.

TED. What?

OLIVER. Oh, I thought that was an apology.

TED. Really.

OLIVER. I thought that's what you were leading up to. I mean, you did the confessional part – the acknowledgment of responsibility for past crimes –

TED. "Crimes?"

OLIVER. – so I thought next we were going to get contrition.

TED. "I'm sorry. Forgive me?" That sort of thing?

OLIVER. In that general neighborhood.

TED. You think I owe you one?

OLIVER. I think it's possible you might think so.

TED. Because of how much I've learned in the meantime? How much I've grown?

OLIVER. I hope we've *all* grown. Jesus, what's the point if we haven't? You know, what have we been doing?

TED. Can I get back to you on that?

OLIVER. Sure.

TED. Is that something you want? An apology?

OLIVER. Doesn't make any difference.

TED. How's your drink?

OLIVER. Fine.

(**TED** *pours a little more into* **OLIVER***'s glass. A beat.*)

TED. But that wasn't why you came?

OLIVER. Nope.

TED. Hoping that you and I would – Maybe after all these years, some satisfaction –

OLIVER. I didn't come with any expectations. I just –

TED. You just came.

OLIVER. Something else I was supposed to do fell out at the last minute, I remember the reunion is happening this weekend, so why not? And I'm glad I did. I really am.

TED. You probably haven't thought about me in years anyway, right? Who the hell am I, anyway? You've got enough people to fill your mind without dredging me up. More pressing things to occupy your – Screenings. Parties. Stuff to crank out for that newspaper of yours. Celebrities to interview.

OLIVER. You make it sound so impressive.

TED. Maybe it isn't impressive in New York or L.A. Maybe it's something people are used to there. Like you run into Woody Allen waiting his turn for his prescription at Walgreen's. Sinus medication, don't you think?

OLIVER. Good chance.

TED. And there's Kim Basinger telling the laundry to be careful with her lingerie.

OLIVER. Yeah, she's a stickler about that.

TED. Maybe, L.A., New York, living with these people as your neighbors, swimming in the same goldfish bowl, it's not such a big deal. But out here in the boonies – in flyover land –

OLIVER. Flyover –

TED. Isn't that what you people call us? You people who live on the coast, one of the coasts. Flyovers? On your way, back and forth between L.A. and New York, we're the ones living down here in places you'd never even think of actually touching down and visiting.

OLIVER. Hey, am I here, am I visiting?

TED. I'm not criticizing.

OLIVER. "Flyover." What a crummy word.

TED. Isn't that one that you people use?

OLIVER. I'm not a "people." I'm just me. And no, I don't use it. I mean, the whole idea of it – talk about condescending.

TED. But don't words happen because they're needed? Something exists, if you want to talk about it, you got to put some sounds together that mean that thing. The word exists because the idea, the attitude exists.

OLIVER. OK, maybe there are some jerks who think like that, who would make up a word like that. But the idea, that you can just discount most of this country, most of the people in this country –

TED. It offends you.

OLIVER. It does.

TED. All right, but let's just take a look at a couple of things that are true. Most of the stuff on TV, in the movies, where is that made? L.A., right? Most of it. OK, maybe every now and then someone says, "What do you say we put a car chase in a cornfield," and so they haul out a map of Kansas, and they sail in and for five or six days, they stay in the local Holiday Inn and complain how they can't find a decent bagel anywhere.

OLIVER. I don't defend behavior like that.

TED. And where are most of the decisions made?

OLIVER. People make decisions everywhere.

TED. I'm talking about the ones that have an effect. How many decisions made here in Ohio are going to change anything about your life? Like what the interest rate is gonna be if you want to take out a home equity loan or something?

OLIVER. Well, interest rates – that's pretty much the Fed, isn't it? In D.C.

TED. D.C. – they're part of the flyover club, too. D.C., L.A., N.Y. Do you think the people who live in these places give a damn the effect of what they decide or do on people they never see?

OLIVER. But not everybody you're talking about is from those places. I mean take Clinton, for instance – he's from Arkansas.

TED. Yeah, the important word there is "from." Do you think –, when his second term's up, when he's finished being President – you think that's where he's going to go live? Clinton? I'm betting L.A. Hell, you're "from" Ohio. Does that make you an Ohioan?

OLIVER. Well, obviously something resonates. I'm here this weekend.

TED. OK, you and some of the others, I'll give you that you may have *started out* in other places. But if you're making the decisions – government, the media – like I said, it's D.C., L.A., NY. And you visiting here, this is not the rule. This is the exception. Not that I'm claiming there's any reason you or any of the others *should* visit. What the hell is here anyway? And whatever there *was* here, there's even less of it now so there's even less reason to come here. Or stay here. Which goes a long way to explaining why we don't bump into Woody Allen or Kim Basinger on Main Street.

OLIVER. Well, I don't see what that has to do with me. I'm not Woody Allen, I'm not Kim Basinger –

TED. You spend time with these people.

OLIVER. I'm just, for professional reasons, sometimes in the same place.

TED. But they look at you. They see that you are there. You are real to them. You have their attention.

OLIVER. But it's not because of *me*. It's not that they're talking to me, really. They're talking to who I write for, and because I do the TV thing. And that I write reviews and they'd like me to like them so when I write about them I'll want to say nice things. I'm an instrument they talk through to get publicity. But don't confuse me with these people. I'm not one of them.

TED. OK.

OLIVER. You don't sound convinced.

TED. *(shrugging in response)* Why *did* you come? You had a free weekend, you say. Why'd you decide to spend it here?

OLIVER. Same reason you did probably. High school. Wherever you go, you carry that with you, right?

TED. Like the clap.

OLIVER. Oh, come on.

TED. No, you're right. High school.

OLIVER. A chance to see old friends.

TED. Did you have friends? At Buchanan High?

OLIVER. Actually, you'd be surprised.

TED. I probably would. No, I'm not being fair.

OLIVER. And I think it's one of the ways you measure stuff, how far you've gone. Or haven't.

TED. Then I'm shit out of luck. I haven't moved two miles.

OLIVER. Not just geographically. There are other kinds of progress. Other measurements.

TED. So you came to measure yourself?

OLIVER. That's probably part of it. But it's always there, isn't it? Who you were. So you go to one of these things, and go into the gym and you see the crepe paper – I mean, my God – *crepe* paper. How many years since I actually saw crepe paper close up –

TED. Real thrill, hunh?

OLIVER. – and there they are – all these people who haven't seen you since you were who you were. Sometimes you can almost read their minds when they see you. "Oh, his skin finally cleared up. Isn't that nice?"

TED. "Oh, he's not serving time."

OLIVER. And maybe you show up just to show that you're around *to* show up.

TED. Yeah?

OLIVER. You know what I'm saying?

TED. No.

OLIVER. Well –

TED. I'm fucking with you, man. Of course I do.

OLIVER. But to say – "See, I exist beyond what you thought I was in high school. I own a car. I have a bank account. I'm not a virgin anymore."

TED. No kidding, that's great news.

OLIVER. To say I've escaped the bounds of who you thought I was, what you thought I was back then.

TED. Well, just the fact that you're alive I consider a victory.

OLIVER. Oh?

TED. You attracted people like me to beat up on you in high school. I figured that in the larger world there would be larger people out there to beat up on you.

OLIVER. There were. There are.

TED. But you're not dead. No, that's great. Maybe I'll take a little credit for that.

OLIVER. I'm listening.

TED. You know in the movies: the son-of-a-bitch sergeant who rode your ass, and you hated his guts, but he toughened you up so you wouldn't get your head blown off in battle. Like I was your own personal one-man boot camp.

OLIVER. Or like a vaccine.

TED. How?

OLIVER. I can't remember which one – Salk, Sabin? One of them, they inject you with weakened polio. A weakened version of the disease. It stimulates the immune system. Builds up your antibodies so later you're ready to take on something stronger.

TED. So I helped you build up your antibodies? I'm a weak version of a disease?

OLIVER. It's an analogy.

TED. No, I'm glad if I was useful. But you know what was going on.

OLIVER. When?

TED. Back in high school. I mean it was obvious. Here you were, you were making your grades and writing for the school paper and winning prizes and scrolls and things. And I knew where you were going.

OLIVER. Where was I going?

TED. Where you went. Out of here.

OLIVER. That made you angry?

TED. And I knew I was going to end up staying, probably working at the plant. Which I did. I'm not complaining. But I would have liked – it would have been nice to have a choice.

OLIVER. Why didn't you go to college? Ohio State.

TED. Right. Could you see me in college?

OLIVER. Why not? You could still – if you wanted to. A lot of people do. Mid-career schooling.

TED. I don't have a career, Oliver. I *work*. We could use some lights.

(TED turns on the deck lights. As the scene progresses, it will get darker in the area off the deck. TED is about to refill OLIVER's glass, when –)

OLIVER. I have to ask –

(He stops.)

TED. Ask. What?

OLIVER. What do you want?

TED. Do I have some kind of agenda?

OLIVER. *Do* you?

TED. Of course.

OLIVER. I mean, inviting me here, your place –

TED. They're opening a new Taco Bell in town, and a letter of recommendation from someone of your stature would be real –

OLIVER. Sure. You got it.

(TED pours, OLIVER drinks. TED starts lighting citronella candles.)

TED. No, I can understand why that's something you'd ask. My intentions. My motives. I can see why you'd be – I'm surprised you took me up on coming here.

OLIVER. You think after all this time, that I would – ?

TED. Maybe. Sure, you could. You'd have a right to.

OLIVER. Well, no. I mean, come on. What would be the point?

TED. Do people always do things because they have points?

OLIVER. I like to think *I* do. I like to think that my life is built on some rational basis.

TED. Well then, good for you.

OLIVER. But, hell, we really aren't the same people. Twenty-five years. Don't the scientists say that all the cells in our body are regenerated every seven years?

TED. Regenerated?

OLIVER. Replaced. New version of the cell comes along, taps the old one on the shoulder. "Hi, I'm here. You can go die now." And so every seven years, you're a whole new you.

TED. Then the me that gave you shit was three or four versions back.

OLIVER. There you go.

TED. Hey, if you think of it that way, nobody should be sentenced to more than seven years in jail. Seven years would make you a lifer.

OLIVER. I think you're on to something.

TED. After seven years, no matter what you've done, you can say that wasn't me that did that rotten thing. That stuff was done by my bad old cells. They're all gone now. I've got me nothing but new, good-guy cells now. Of course, you want to work on it that your new cells really are an improvement. Don't want to have a lot of back-sliding cells fucking up your progress.

OLIVER. Sure, got to be vigilant.

TED. Though, today, at the lunch – looked to me like some of the gang, their new cells were major back-sliders.

OLIVER. Mitch?

TED. Oh, man, you ever see anything so pathetic?

OLIVER. What happened?

TED. A major taste for the booze has to be part of it.

OLIVER. But you don't know?

TED. Haven't seen him in years.

OLIVER. You used to hang out, I thought –

TED. No. Not for years. I think he lives in Cleveland. Not a place I get to.

OLIVER. When you think of what he used to –

TED. He did not get good replacement cells. You like Bruce Willis?

OLIVER. He's done some good work.

TED. You ever meet him?

OLIVER. Did an interview once.

TED. You know what gets me? When he was still with Demi Moore. Between them, they must have had all the money in the world. And he still let her take her clothes off so everyone could see. You tell me how that's different from Larry Axelrod, this guy I used to work with at the plant, carries a picture of his wife in his wallet. Lying naked on the pool table in his rec room. "Like to see what I got?" This expression on her face of, "Take the goddamn picture already, will you?" And he pulls this out, says, "This is mine. You can look, but you can't touch. *I'm* the only one gets to touch." Like I would want to, you know? You see her in the supermarket, trying to decide which brand of spaghetti sauce to buy. I have to keep myself from saying, "Lady, I've seen your bush."

OLIVER. Hmmmm.

TED. So how is he different from Bruce Willis? When he was married to –

OLIVER. Demi?

TED. He'd go to a premiere of one of her movies. All these stars around them – Danny DeVito, Sharon Stone, Denzel Washington – the media, sitting there in a crowded theatre, and up there was Demi – forty feet high. Some actor putting his hands all over her. End of the movie, lights come up, Bruce probably gave her a kiss, said, "Good work, honey."

OLIVER. Well, he did them, too. Nude scenes.

TED. I think people like them – they do it to piss us off.

OLIVER. I'm sorry, people like who, do what?

TED. Like Larry Axelrod and Willis. The whole "look, but don't touch" thing. Of course, there's a difference, depending where you are on the – you know – scale.

OLIVER. Scale?

TED. If you're a guy on the street in a raincoat and you flash, you get arrested. If you do it at like one of those topless clubs out by the airport, you're this pathetic thing one step up from a hooker. But if you're Bruce or Demi or Sharon Stone or Michael Douglas and you get paid seven million dollars and wave your stuff around, you can pretend you're an artist. And people wonder what's wrong with this country. Another?

OLIVER. Hunh? Sure.

(**TED** *starts to make him another drink.*)

TED. I'm gonna have to go inside, get some more ice.

OLIVER. That's OK.

TED. It's not a problem.

IRIS. *(from offstage)* Hello?

TED. Yes?

IRIS. *(offstage)* Ted?

TED. Back here! Iris?

IRIS. *(offstage)* Yes.

TED. In the back. The deck.

(**IRIS** *appears.*)

Look at you.

IRIS. The girl I thought I was going to have to fill in for – her shift –

*(aside to **OLIVER**)*

A restaurant.

(**OLIVER** *nods his comprehension.*)

TED. She showed up after all?

IRIS. I guess she's feeling better. Or she needs the money. Something.

TED. Well, that's good news.

IRIS. Yeah, except, of course, I could use the money, too.

TED. How much you need?

IRIS. You got a spare seven or eight grand?

TED. I left my checkbook in my other life. What about you, Oliver?

IRIS. Don't you go giving Oliver shit.

TED. Actually, I was gonna get more ice for his drink. You want something?

IRIS. Well, I wouldn't say no to a Scotch rocks.

TED. Your turn to get waited on, hunh?

(**TED** *exits.*)

IRIS. Same old Ted.

OLIVER. Oh, I don't know. I think he's –

IRIS. What?

OLIVER. Matured.

IRIS. Matured? Ted?

OLIVER. Well, he hasn't broken my glasses yet.

IRIS. You aren't wearing glasses.

OLIVER. He's being friendly.

IRIS. He ask you for money?

OLIVER. Does he need money?

IRIS. Oliver, everybody in this town needs money.

OLIVER. I didn't realize things were so depressed here.

IRIS. Take a look over there. See that building?

OLIVER. That's the plant –

IRIS. You see any lights in the windows?

OLIVER. *(understands)* Ah. What happened?

IRIS. Some conglomerate bought the plant. Eltar. We were going to be a division of Eltar. "The world at your doorstep through electronics."

OLIVER. Seems to me if the world were at your doorstep, it would be pretty hard to open the door.

IRIS. We were going to be a division. Part of Eltar's big happy extended corporate family. And then someone in New York looked at a balance sheet and I guess figured out that there was fifty cents to be saved by shutting the plant down. So much for family feeling.

OLIVER. When did this happen?

IRIS. When did it finally shut down? About seven months ago.

OLIVER. I didn't know.

IRIS. Stuff people used to do over there, now's being done in Malaysia. Is it Malaysia or Malaya?

OLIVER. Malaysia sounds right. I think it's on the Malay peninsula.

IRIS. Where is that?

OLIVER. Somewhere east is all I know.

IRIS. Well, somewhere east a bunch of Malaysians are plugging components into boards that people here used to plug. Hunh.

OLIVER. What?

IRIS. You came back. You actually came back.

OLIVER. Why is everyone so surprised I came back?

IRIS. I saw a documentary on TV. On PBS probably. Yes, I sometimes watch PBS. This woman – this Jewish woman – she's visiting the concentration camp she was in during World War II. She's taking these filmmakers around. Showing where all this stuff happened to her, to people she knew. Where people died. Her sister. I couldn't understand that either.

OLIVER. There *is* a difference between Buchanan High and Auschwitz. A pretty crucial one actually.

IRIS. What I said was dumb.

OLIVER. I didn't mean to jump on you.

IRIS. No, you're right.

OLIVER. I was rude.

IRIS. And that's the worst thing that ever happened to me. Forget it.

OLIVER. I really didn't have that bad a time here. Everybody thinks I was miserable here.

IRIS. You enjoyed being beaten up?

OLIVER. Oh, kids get beaten up everywhere.

IRIS. Doesn't mean that it was right for them to do that to you.

OLIVER. No permanent damage.

IRIS. Do you remember who I am?

OLIVER. Iris.

IRIS. He called me that. If he hadn't, would you have – Do you remember *me?*

OLIVER. You used to go with the drummer.

IRIS. You *do* remember!

OLIVER. What was his name – Ken? He used to carry his sticks with him and drum on his desk top in study hall.

IRIS. Yeah, I could pick 'em, couldn't I?

OLIVER. Sure, I remember you.

   *(**TED** returns with a tray, carrying drinks and munchies. He serves in a parody of a cocktail waitress.)*

TED. Here we go –

IRIS. What is that? That you're doing?

TED. The bunny dip.

IRIS. What the hell is that?

TED. It's how they served drinks at the Playboy Club. The girls. They had ears that they wore, and tails on their behinds and they would serve like this.

IRIS. I'm sure I wouldn't know.

TED. I was in the club in Chicago once. Back when I was I don't know how young. Somebody's uncle took us. We were impressed, I've got to tell you.

IRIS. Wow, real live women with actual breasts.

TED. Yeah, those were pretty much my thoughts.

IRIS. If you want to get technical, they probably weren't actual breasts.

TED. I think the tails were real, though.

OLIVER. I hope so.

IRIS. *Some*thing to believe in, hunh?

TED. Tell you the truth, I was hoping to meet your wife. See what she looks like.

OLIVER. A real live woman with actual breasts.

TED. No tail?

OLIVER. Probably had the operation before I met her.

TED. A little scar at the base of the spine?

IRIS. You're both amusing the hell out of me.

TED. Are we being gross, Iris?

OLIVER. No, she's right.

TED. Iris has delicate sensibilities, don't you?

IRIS. Yeah, I blush easy.

TED. *(toasting)* To fellow veterans –

*(They join him in the toast. **OLIVER**'s pager goes off. **OLIVER** reaches into his jacket pocket and pulls it out.)*

What is that – a pager?

OLIVER. Sorry.

TED. What's to be sorry about? You're a busy guy, an important guy.

OLIVER. Mind if I use your phone?

TED. Down the hall, the room on the left. A little privacy.

OLIVER. Sorry. I'll charge it to my credit –

TED. No, fine.

*(**OLIVER** goes into the house. **TED** turns to **IRIS**.)*

I didn't think you were going to join us.

IRIS. I didn't think I was either.

TED. What changed your mind?

IRIS. Who says it's changed?

TED. You're here.

IRIS. You know what your problem is?

TED. My problem is people keep telling me what my problem is. Like I give a shit about their opinion.

IRIS. Fine.

TED. I'm sorry, Iris. Were you about to give me constructive criticism? Were you about to tell me something that if I took it to heart it would turn my whole life around?

IRIS. Far be it from me –

TED. I hope so. I should fucking hope so –

IRIS. Maybe I'll just finish my drink and go.

TED. Do what you want to do.

IRIS. I don't need this.

TED. No, you just need, what is it – seven or eight grand?

IRIS. You assume the whole world is like you –

TED. I assume that people have needs and will do what they have to to meet them.

IRIS. Yeah, but there are limits.

TED. When did you start teaching Sunday school?

IRIS. Fine. How's your wife?

TED. What's that supposed to mean?

IRIS. Why does it have to mean anything more than the words I use?

TED. What's her name?

IRIS. Lianne.

TED. So why don't you say that? Why don't you ask, "How's Lianne?" How's my wife.

IRIS. Fine. How's Lianne?

TED. She's visiting her mother. She and the kids.

IRIS. So she's not around.

TED. No. Did you want to have a conversation with her?

IRIS. Conversation?

TED. Did you want to do some heart-to-heart feminine thing? Bonding?

IRIS. Right. I want her to tell me all of your secrets.

TED. And what would you do with them?

IRIS. I'd use them against you, of course. I would conspire with your enemies and I'd bring you down. God, do you know the meaning of the word "paranoid"?

TED. OK.

IRIS. Can't I express concern?

TED. Is that what you were doing?

IRIS. "How's Lianne?" Yes, I think so.

TED. All right, sorry. I'm an asshole again. Sorry. She's – what am I going to say? "She's fine?"

IRIS. Anyway, I wouldn't bond with her. I think that's what *men* do. They bond.

TED. What do women do?

IRIS. Confide, console.

TED. Well, what if *I* want to confide and console?

IRIS. Who to? Another guy?

TED. I'm not saying I'm actually thinking of doing this –

IRIS. I think if you were going to confide and console with another guy it would probably be read as bonding.

TED. I just want to know how this works.

IRIS. I'm not an expert.

TED. But Iris –

IRIS. What?

TED. If you ever catch me consoling or confiding or bonding with some guy –

IRIS. Unh-hunh?

TED. I want you to shoot me. Right here.

IRIS. But not otherwise?

TED. Fuck you, too.

(She laughs. A beat.)

IRIS. I heard some talk – did you hear this – ?

TED. You have to tell me before I can say yes or no.

IRIS. Right.

TED. I don't read minds.

IRIS. Just that there's some talk about putting together some deal to buy the plant back.

TED. Oh yeah, yeah –

IRIS. I mean it sounded serious. There are other places where people – the employees – they bought back their company.

TED. I'm supposed to help buy back the company? Quick, let me cash in all my vast portfolio of stocks and bonds.

IRIS. I think they did this up in Dayton.

TED. It's easy to talk.

IRIS. What I hear is that there's some serious possibility. What's-his-name, the union –

TED. Dunphy?

IRIS. The other one.

TED. Stetlano.

IRIS. Stetlano, yes. Word is Stetlano says there's some interested money. It would mean new contracts, but basically we'd be working for ourselves.

TED. Oh, don't kid yourself. Somebody would still have the power to hire and fire. Somebody would still make policy. Decide whether to change the shape of the buttons or what color plastic would be used in the shell. You'd still have to keep somebody above you happy.

IRIS. Do you prefer unemployment?

TED. I'm not saying that. But whenever you have to answer to somebody else, there's always somebody else you've got to –

IRIS. – to answer to?

TED. Unless you work for yourself. Like make pottery in the basement.

IRIS. Well, there's your answer. Get yourself a potter's wheel –

TED. A what?

IRIS. That's what they make pottery on. A wheel. Didn't you ever see *Ghost?*

TED. The movie?

IRIS. Demi Moore. She's making pottery. She's got a potter's wheel.

TED. Is this before or after she takes off her clothes?

IRIS. I don't think she does it in that one.

TED. Too bad.

IRIS. Who cares? God, do you think of anything else?

TED. I'd tell you only I'm afraid you'd think I was confiding.

IRIS. I thought you would find it interesting, is all. I mean, if they can pull this thing together at the plant –

TED. – when it happens, they can call me. If my phone hasn't been disconnected.

IRIS. Giving up isn't the answer.

TED. I'm not giving up. But I'm not gonna hold my breath.

(**OLIVER** *returns.*)

What was it – L.A. or New York? That called?

OLIVER. New York.

TED. Everything OK?

OLIVER. Scheduling. Someone had to change a date on me. Studio wants some retakes on this picture, that means someone I was supposed to interview –

TED. An actor?

OLIVER. Actress. She isn't going to be in the country when we were scheduled to talk. So we have to figure out another time. So her people call my people –

IRIS. You have "people"?

OLIVER. In the office.

TED. You and your people – you have a flag? An anthem?

OLIVER. I should look into that.

TED. T-shirts, sweatshirts –

OLIVER. Actually, they're employed by the production company. The TV show. As I am. And Sarah. So I don't hire them so much as they're hired to help me.

TED. You all call each other by your first names?

OLIVER. Sure. Why not?

TED. So you're *good* to your people.

OLIVER. I try to be good *with* them.

TED. "With," not "to."

OLIVER. Yes.

(He has reached into the jacket draped over the chair and taken an electronic organizer out of his pocket and starts typing.)

TED. You're a walking electronics outlet – The pager, this –

OLIVER. It's how I keep my schedule straight. And, you know, appointments and addresses and phone numbers.

TED. How many numbers can it hold?

OLIVER. A few thousand, I guess.

TED. You know that many people?

OLIVER. I didn't say I filled it all.

TED. Put me in there. Me and Iris. We want to be in your organizer.

IRIS. Speak for yourself.

TED. You don't want to be in Oliver's organizer? You too good to be in Oliver's –

IRIS. Oliver hasn't invited me to be in his organizer.

OLIVER. You want to be in my organizer?

IRIS. OK now –

OLIVER. McCarty, right? Iris McCarty?

IRIS. You don't have to.

OLIVER. Let me just get to the M's.

(He fiddles with the keyboard.)

IRIS. It's really –

OLIVER. No, I think it – There we go. McCarty. M-C. not M-A-C, right?

IRIS. Right.

OLIVER. Here.

(He offers it to her.)

IRIS. I should type it in?

OLIVER. Why not?

IRIS. All right.

(She starts typing her particulars in.)

What do I do now?

OLIVER. Just hit "save." Right there, see?

(She does it.)

TED. My turn, my turn!

*(**OLIVER** hands the organizer over to **TED**.)*

Jeez, you need fingers like, what's his name, the guy from *Fantasy Island*? "The plane, the plane!"

OLIVER. If you want me to type it –

TED. No, I can do it.

(He types.)

Well, I guess this is possible.

OLIVER. I wouldn't want to write a long article on it.

TED. *(pressing a button)* Save.

(**TED** *doesn't hand it back to* **OLIVER.**)

So, who we in there with?

OLIVER. Oh – my accountant. The liquor store. Bruce Taybor, my producer.

TED. Sarah –

OLIVER. Yes, Sarah's in there.

TED. John Travolta?

OLIVER. No.

TED. If I look under "T" in here, I wouldn't find John Travolta's home number?

OLIVER. No.

TED. But there are famous people in here. People I've heard of.

OLIVER. Mostly their offices. Maybe their managers.

TED. How do you like that, Iris? We're in the same organizer as some famous people's managers.

IRIS. You want to give that back to him?

TED. I'm sorry, of course.

(tosses it back to **OLIVER***)*

Probably a lot of Jewish names in there, too, right?

IRIS. Oh, for God's sake!

TED. I'm not saying anything!

IRIS. "A lot of Jewish names" and you aren't saying anything?

TED. What, there aren't a lot of Jewish people in show business? You're gonna tell me there aren't a lot of Jewish people in show business? Oliver, you're Jewish, right?

OLIVER. Yes.

TED. You're in show business, right?

OLIVER. Yes.

TED. A lot of the people you know in show business –

OLIVER. – a lot of them are Jewish, too, yes, so?

TED. So nothing. It's just an observation. There's something about being Jewish, probably, that – probably some cultural thing about talent. A lot of the comedians, standups –

OLIVER. Yes.

TED. Paul Newman –

IRIS. He is?

TED. You didn't know that?

IRIS. No.

TED. Everybody knows that. Tell her I'm right.

OLIVER. He's right.

TED. Paul Newman's Jewish. You know who isn't, though – I read this, I didn't believe it but it's true –

OLIVER. Tell us.

TED. Rod Steiger.

OLIVER. I didn't know that.

TED. How about that? I know something you don't know. About your own business.

IRIS. Are you sure?

TED. Surprising, isn't it? You'd think if *anybody* –

IRIS. And so how does this change your world, your life?

TED. Not saying it does. It's just interesting. It just goes to show you that your prejudices, your stereotypes, things aren't what you – You see what I'm getting at, don't you, Oliver?

OLIVER. Yes.

TED. Just because Steiger's played pawnbrokers and Mexican bandits and stuff doesn't mean he's necessarily Jewish.

IRIS. Why would playing Mexican bandits mean you're Jewish?

TED. Because they do a lot. Eli Wallach.

OLIVER. Actually, here's how it works, Ted – if you're in my organizer, you're automatically Jewish.

TED. Hey, cool.

OLIVER. That's how it works.

TED. Well, I'm honored.

OLIVER. The yarmulke will arrive in the mail. Allow ten business days for delivery.

IRIS. *(holding up her glass)* You mind if I – ?

TED. Help yourself. Naw, a lot of the most talented people –

IRIS. You still on that?

TED. I think it's interesting. Spielberg, Woody Allen, Streisand. Though, jeez, did you see that Streisand special, couple of years ago? She's up there singing. Madison Square Garden, Vegas or someplace. But she's up there singing, and there are these shots in the audience. And there are all of these shots of, like, old boyfriends. Maybe Ryan O'Neal, that hairdresser guy, I think, Elliot Gould –

OLIVER. – another Jew –

TED. Yeah, but that's not my point. It was like, let's look at the club. You know, the club of people who had things with Barbra Streisand. And she's up there singing, a love song probably. And smiling while she's singing, and in the audience there are these people who are veterans of Barbra. But they're looking up at her as she sings this song. Maybe a song of eternal love or something. To people she's mostly dumped. But I guess if you're part of that scene, it's kind of expected of you.

OLIVER. Expected?

TED. That after a couple of years you'll co-star opposite someone else, do a love scene – a nude scene – and switch to *them*. People would be disappointed if you didn't. These people get married – the question isn't if they'll break up, but when. Sometimes, you know, I think, *I* could do famous better than some of them. You wouldn't see *me* in embarrassing headlines, the checkout line at the grocery. Punching out photographers, racking up frequent flyer mileage at Betty Ford –

IRIS. You talk a lot of shit, you know that?

TED. You think so?

IRIS. I'm saying it, aren't I?

TED. You think I'm wrong?

IRIS. Right, wrong – what does it matter? Why are you talking about this? Celebrities for God's sake –

TED. Don't forget, you're talking in front of a guy who makes his living –

OLIVER. No, I actually kind of agree.

TED. That I talk a lot of shit?

OLIVER. That celebrities – they really aren't that significant.

TED. But it's what you spend your life –

OLIVER. I review movies and sometimes I do interviews. And I have fun, sure, sometimes, but it's not like this is important. Not seriously.

TED. So you're doing something that isn't important. Your work, it isn't –

OLIVER. Well, I guess people have to have some diversion. I guess that serves a function. But no, compared to the real stuff –

TED. Politics –

OLIVER. The real issues –

TED. The spotted crane, civil rights, the national debt –

OLIVER. All that –

TED. So why do you do it?

OLIVER. It's what I do.

TED. But if it isn't important –

OLIVER. It's what I do. It's what someone is willing to pay me for. People end up in jobs and, Ted, that's what they *do*. Their *jobs*. Their work. They get salaries, to earn them, they do their work –

TED. *(with heat)* If they *have* work. If they're lucky enough to *have* salaries. If they're lucky enough to have jobs they get paid salaries to hang around with famous people in New York and L.A. and make judgments like nobody else is entitled to have an opinion.

(a beat)

OLIVER. *(rising)* Maybe it's time for me to –

TED. No, please look, I – apologize. I just – Please. You know, this kind of – it means something to me. You visiting like this. Because, yeah, it's bothered me.

OLIVER. What?

TED. You think I don't look back, I don't know what I was? How rotten I –

OLIVER. Hey, I already said –

TED. Yeah, but it's not only what *you* say, it's how I feel about *myself*. So, please –

(LIANNE enters from around the side of the house. She carries a large stamp album. She looks at OLIVER, her mouth open.)

OLIVER. But it's getting late, and there are things I want to do tomorrow. Other people I want to catch up with. Some sleep –

(Now OLIVER sees her.)

Hello?

(TED turns and sees LIANNE.)

LIANNE. Where's your wife?

TED. Honey?

OLIVER. My wife?

TED. What are you doing here, honey?

LIANNE. I see you with her all the time.

OLIVER. You see me – ?

TED. She's confused. She means Sarah. On TV.

OLIVER. Oh.

TED. *(to LIANNE)* That's not his wife.

LIANNE. Sure, she talks like –

TED. No, honey, that's someone else. That's a friend of his.

LIANNE. Oh.

TED. Somebody who works with him.

OLIVER. But a lot of people make that mistake. It's OK.

TED. It's an actress.

OLIVER. Well, not an actress exactly –

TED. But not a real person –

LIANNE. But, the way you talk to each other –

OLIVER. Yes, well –

LIANNE. The way you fight –

TED. They don't fight.

OLIVER. Does it look like we're fighting?

TED. She gets confused.

> *(to* **LIANNE***)*
>
> Lianne, honey, what are you doing here? You're supposed to be with your mama today.
>
> *(to* **OLIVER***)*
>
> Her mother lives at the other end of the development. About a half mile down that –

LIANNE. I took a walk.

TED. But, Lianne, that's not what you were supposed to do. You and the boys were supposed to visit with your mama today. Remember?

LIANNE. She fell asleep – Mama. We were watching something and –

TED. – she fell asleep?

LIANNE. They all did. The boys, too.

> *(to* **OLIVER***)*
>
> We have two boys.
>
> *(to* **TED***)*
>
> We were all watching this movie. It was old. They fell asleep. Black and white. The people in it are all dead. God, you forget how many dead people there are.

TED. A lot of them.

LIANNE. Seems like there didn't used to be so many. Or is it me? It must be me. You didn't say you were going to have a party.

TED. This isn't a party. We're just –

OLIVER. I'm Oliver.

LIANNE. I know. The TV.

OLIVER. And you're – Lianne, is it?

LIANNE. He's my wife. I mean, I'm his –

OLIVER. Oh. Well, hello.

LIANNE. Stupid.

OLIVER. No. Anybody can get confused. I get confused all the time. I'm confused right now.

IRIS. How are you, Lianne?

LIANNE. Iris.

IRIS. You want to come sit down?

TED. Tell you what I'm worried about – if your mama wakes up and finds out that you're gone? She'll wonder. She'll be concerned.

LIANNE. But I'm with you.

TED. She doesn't know that.

LIANNE. You could call.

TED. But then I'd wake her maybe.

LIANNE. If she's asleep then she's not worried.

TED. But she might wake up. Or the boys. They're gonna wake up.

LIANNE. Well, that's OK – they're at Grandma's. I'm thirsty.

(a beat)

TED. I'll get you a coke.

LIANNE. That's not what *you're* drinking.

TED. Do you want the coke?

LIANNE. I'm just saying –

TED. *Do* you want the coke? Honey, do you want the coke?

(a beat)

LIANNE. Sure. Yes.

(She drifts onto the deck as **OLIVER** *remains standing.* **TED** *fetches the coke for her.)*

OLIVER. You weren't at the luncheon today.

LIANNE. No, I was over at Mama's.

TED. Lianne mostly doesn't know the people I went to high school with. And she gets a little nervous in crowds.

LIANNE. Too many people, they use up the air. That's not scientific, I know, but it feels like it.

OLIVER. Yes, I've noticed that.

LIANNE. So I'm not crazy.

OLIVER. What's that you've got there? The book?

LIANNE. Oh, this, yes. Ted, I think this is it.

TED. *(handing her a coke)* What's that?

LIANNE. This is – I was going through some of my dad's stuff in the basement –

(to **OLIVER***)*

My dad died a month ago?

OLIVER. I'm sorry.

LIANNE. He was a real good man. I miss him a lot. But I was going through some of his stuff. Mama was asleep and I found this in a box, and I thought maybe it could be –

TED. *What* could it be?

LIANNE. *(to* **OLIVER***)* Do you know anything about stamps?

OLIVER. You mean, to collect?

LIANNE. Some of them are valuable. I know this. Some stamps. I've heard –

OLIVER. I think you're right. Yes. The rare ones can be – some of them can go for –

LIANNE. How much?

OLIVER. Well, different stamps, different prices. And, you know, collectors –

LIANNE. If you have a stamp that a collector wants –

OLIVER. Sure, some of them, thousands of dollars. Tens of thousands even. Depending on how rare, what condition they're in, whether they're postmarked –

LIANNE. Postmarked is when there are black lines on them?

OLIVER. Right. Means that they've been –

LIANNE. Used?

OLIVER. Used, yes, right. Cancelled. You see a stamp that's got those black, wavy lines on it –

LIANNE. Maybe *I* should wear some black, wavy lines –

OLIVER. Oh?

LIANNE. 'Cross my forehead. What, do you think it would catch on?

TED. Lianne –

LIANNE. So serious, so serious. But cancelled is no good?

OLIVER. It's *less* good. Like I say, the better the condition –

LIANNE. Of course.

OLIVER. Mint condition is best.

LIANNE. You know more about stamps than you said.

OLIVER. No, just a little. When I was a kid.

LIANNE. You collected stamps?

OLIVER. Nine or ten years old. God knows where they are now.

LIANNE. Would you mind taking a look?

TED. I'm sorry, Oliver, you shouldn't have to –

LIANNE. He can say no if he wants to.

OLIVER. It's OK, Ted.

TED. You didn't come out here to appraise –

OLIVER. Actually, I'm kind of interested.

*(**LIANNE** hands **OLIVER** the stamp album. **OLIVER** begins to look through it.)*

LIANNE. Cuz it would be great if you saw anything that was actually worth something in there. Something that we could sell.

OLIVER. Ah.

LIANNE. We're broke, you know.

TED. Lianne!

*(to **OLIVER**)*

We're not broke.

LIANNE. But why we can't get the dryer repaired?

TED. The guy doesn't have time for an appointment another couple of weeks.

LIANNE. Oh, then I got it wrong.

TED. I'm in-between jobs, is all. So's half the town. Christ, you make it sound like it's time to invest in a tin cup.

OLIVER. Hey, it's happening everywhere. Downsizing.

IRIS. Don't you love that word?

OLIVER. I have writer friends, they can't understand how if there's eighty-million cable channels to choose from, how come they can't get work.

TED. Somebody has to write that stuff Peter Graves says. Or the narration, the *National Geographic*.

OLIVER. A lot of the channels, they're putting on old shows. Or documentaries of World War II.

TED. So they're not hiring actors.

OLIVER. I guess not.

TED. What do you need someone to play Hitler for some TV movie, when you've got all that stuff of the real thing yelling his head off?

LIANNE. Oh, *he's* in here!

TED. Who's where?

LIANNE. *(flipping through pages in the album)* No, see, I'll show you – There, see? Lots of Hitler. German stamps.

TED. Yup, that's Hitler.

LIANNE. They must be worth something, don't you think? Everybody's heard of Hitler.

OLIVER. Well, it isn't really how famous the people on the stamps are. It's how rare.

LIANNE. Oh, so because there's a lot of Hitler stamps –

OLIVER. Right.

LIANNE. OK, this makes sense. I follow this.

OLIVER. *(looking through the book)* You know I remember some of these.

LIANNE. The hinges, they're getting loose –

OLIVER. You know something –

LIANNE. What?

OLIVER. I think this one –

LIANNE. The pink one?

OLIVER. This could be. You might have something here. Yes, I remember. The Springfield commemorative. This is one of the ones I could never get. I saw it in a stamp store once when I was a kid. I was there with my dad. I said, "Dad, this one." He asked how much. I told him. He just laughed, like, "Dream on."

LIANNE. Expensive?

OLIVER. It would have meant a lot of weeks without allowance, let me put it that way. So it's one of the ones I never got. This is in good condition. You should have someone who knows this stuff take a look at it. I mean really knows. Or buy a guide.

LIANNE. There are guides?

OLIVER. Oh yeah – the value of different editions and so forth. I wouldn't be surprised if there's some stuff in here that's really appreciated in value.

LIANNE. Well, that would be real good news.

OLIVER. Actually, you know what?

LIANNE. What?

OLIVER. I'd like to buy that stamp.

LIANNE. The pink one?

OLIVER. Yeah.

TED. Do you collect stamps now?

OLIVER. No. But there's something about – this is one I always wanted. Like an itch I never got to scratch. I told you, my dad –

TED. If you don't collect, what would you do with it?

OLIVER. Maybe put it into one of the little plastic windows in my wallet.

TED. Keepsake kind of thing.

OLIVER. Something I always wanted and there it is. You must know the feeling. When you were a kid, something you wanted, never got.

TED. Sure – a hand grenade.

(He laughs at his own joke.)

OLIVER. You willing to sell?

LIANNE. Why not?

OLIVER. Shall we say a hundred dollars?

LIANNE. Is it worth that much?

OLIVER. It's worth what someone's willing to pay, and I'm willing to pay a hundred dollars.

TED. I guess this is your lucky day, Lianne.

LIANNE. Well, yeah, OK. But that's not why I showed it to you –

OLIVER. I know.

LIANNE. You're our guest. You don't have guests in your house to sell them stuff.

OLIVER. It was my idea, remember. I'd consider it a favor.

TED. Lianne, the man's waiting for you to make a decision.

LIANNE. OK then.

OLIVER. OK?

LIANNE. Yuh.

OLIVER. Good.

(He takes a hundred out of his wallet and gives it to her. Then he delicately takes the stamp out of the book and slides it into his wallet.)

There.

LIANNE. The fastest hundred dollars I ever made.

OLIVER. You're happy, I'm happy. This is a definition of a good deal.

TED. You know what, though, honey –

LIANNE. What?

TED. I think I'd better drive you back to your mom's. Her feelings are going to be awful hurt if she wakes up and you're not there. She's going to think you don't like her.

LIANNE. Oh she knows better –

TED. But still, I think it's a good idea.

LIANNE. Well –

TED. I'll just do that.

    (to **OLIVER** *and* **IRIS***)*

    Give me a minute or two and I'll be back.

OLIVER. It was nice meeting you, Lianne.

LIANNE. You, too.

IRIS. You look pretty today, Lianne.

LIANNE. Oh?

IRIS. I like your hair.

LIANNE. Oh, yours, too.

TED. I'll just be a few minutes.

    *(***TED*** gently escorts* **LIANNE** *off the deck, around the side of the house and offstage. The sound of a car starting and driving away.* **OLIVER** *and* **IRIS** *are alone together.)*

IRIS. She was on good behavior. You should take that as a compliment. Something about you calmed her down. I have to hand it to Ted, his patience. I mean, you saw –

OLIVER. How long – ?

IRIS. Well, she's always been a little unsteady. But it's been worse lately – first, the plant closing, then her father dying. The things that have always been there suddenly not.

OLIVER. Losing a parent is real hard.

IRIS. Your folks?

OLIVER. Both gone. Yours?

IRIS. My dad's still hanging in there. He and an old buddy named Hank and Hank's wife share a place down in the Florida Keys. I went down to visit, and I got the feeling that they'd moved a lot of stuff around before I got there, for my sake.

OLIVER. Cleaned up?

IRIS. More hiding the evidence.

OLIVER. Evidence of what? They running drugs or something?

IRIS. I think when it comes to Hank's wife, it's share and share alike.

OLIVER. Hank's wife puts up with this?

IRIS. Actually, I think it was more or less her idea. Apparently Hank has slowed down some.

OLIVER. Oh.

IRIS. And she hasn't.

OLIVER. And your father?

IRIS. Well, he's always tried to make himself useful.

OLIVER. They didn't want you to know this?

IRIS. I guess they thought I might have opinions.

OLIVER. You don't?

IRIS. At this point in their lives, jeez, if they can put together something that works for them, who am I to –

OLIVER. Sure.

IRIS. Kind of a hoot though, when I think back to how hard I tried to hide the stuff I was doing from *him* – my dad. And that he threw me out of the house for being a tramp.

OLIVER. Did he?

IRIS. Yeah.

OLIVER. That's kind of harsh.

IRIS. Well, I got knocked up. The summer after I got out of high school. He wasn't too happy about that.

OLIVER. Ken the drummer?

IRIS. Somebody else. I was smart enough not to marry him, though. What can I tell you – I was a wild kid. And now my kid's a wild kid. My daughter. Twenty-four now, not such a kid. You're looking at a grandmother.

OLIVER. I don't believe it.

IRIS. You're not the only one. But the same guy, you know – my dad – same guy who gave me grief about what I did back then, now here he is in a seniors threesome. And it seems kind of OK. They're all getting along, nobody's getting hurt –

OLIVER. Maybe different rules apply at different ages. There's stuff that we think is OK for people over eighteen to do that we think twelve year-olds shouldn't. So maybe there's a later stage where stuff that would be upsetting, disturbing in people in their thirties, forties, fifties – maybe there's a point where it starts being almost – cute?

IRIS. That's just the word I want to associate with my sex life. "How's your sex life?" "Cute." You got kids?

OLIVER. Nope.

IRIS. You came here alone. Your wife –

OLIVER. This wouldn't be her scene.

IRIS. She stayed in New York.

OLIVER. My reasons for coming here weren't anything she'd be interested in.

(He gets up and pours himself another drink.)

You want another?

IRIS. Actually, yes, I would.

OLIVER. What about you? Married? Not married?

IRIS. Not.

OLIVER. Not now, or not ever?

IRIS. Both.

OLIVER. Oh. Any particular reason?

IRIS. Not a lot of guys that interested in taking up with you when a baby that isn't theirs is part of the deal.

OLIVER. And when she stopped being a baby?

IRIS. By then I was used to not having someone else underfoot. Don't get the wrong impression –

OLIVER. What impression do you think I'm getting that might be wrong?

IRIS. Skip it.

OLIVER. Why?

IRIS. Oh, it's just a lot of horseshit.

OLIVER. What is?

IRIS. Come on – I say something about my life, you make sounds like you hear me and understand or sympathize, and tomorrow or the day after, you climb back onto a jet and fly to whichever coast and what's the point? That you feel good about yourself?

OLIVER. Why would I feel good about myself?

IRIS. Because you've – you think – you're under the impression that by listening to me you –

OLIVER. I what?

IRIS. – you've done something?

OLIVER. Done what? What have I done?

IRIS. Exactly.

OLIVER. I'm sorry?

IRIS. What *have* you done?

OLIVER. I don't know. You tell me. You've got the floor.

IRIS. Look, why don't I just say to you that I really and truly believe that you are a good guy and the rest of the dance isn't necessary.

OLIVER. But I *am* interested. I wouldn't ask if I weren't.

IRIS. Fine, and what good does that do? You're interested. How does that make either of our lives better? Waste of time, Oliver. Full credit for good intentions, but waste of time.

OLIVER. What are we arguing about?

IRIS. We're not.

OLIVER. Then why do I get the feeling you're mad at me?

IRIS. I'm not.

OLIVER. OK.

IRIS. I'm not mad at you.

OLIVER. OK.

IRIS. Just because I may disagree with you about something, that doesn't mean –

OLIVER. Well, yeah, see that's what I want to know –

IRIS. What?

OLIVER. What we're disagreeing about.

IRIS. Look, are we having a good time?

OLIVER. Yes.

IRIS. So why don't we just have it and not analyze it. This job of yours – this movie reviewing – keep it to the movies. I don't want to worry how many stars you're giving me for this conversation.

OLIVER. I wouldn't do that. I don't do that.

IRIS. Hey, how much is it really worth?

OLIVER. What?

IRIS. The stamp. How much?

OLIVER. Oh, maybe four thousand dollars.

IRIS. Gee, I would have thought more.

OLIVER. Well, maybe I underestimate. Maybe six, seven –

IRIS. Maybe six or seven *cents.*

OLIVER. You think Lianne might have put one over on me?

IRIS. That's right, it was her doing.

OLIVER. *(handing her the drink, smiles)* You were wrong about my not remembering you.

IRIS. Oh?

OLIVER. I think you might be surprised how much I used to think about you –

IRIS. About me how, as if I can't guess.

OLIVER. Well, aside from that.

IRIS. You never said anything.

OLIVER. What was I going to do, ask you for a date?

IRIS. People do. People did.

OLIVER. But there was something about you –

IRIS. What was about me?

OLIVER. This is going to sound sort of –

IRIS. Never mind what it sounds –

OLIVER. I thought – the crowd you hung out with? – I thought you were better than them.

IRIS. Better?

OLIVER. Not to put down the gang you hung out with –

IRIS. Even if they were lowlifes like Ted?

OLIVER. Well – but that there was more there. That you –

IRIS. I wasn't just a wild kid.

OLIVER. There was something –

IRIS. I had potential. I was a diamond in the rough. If you had the nerve, you would have shown me there were better things in life, finer things –

OLIVER. Put it that way, I sound like an asshole.

IRIS. *(waving his comment aside)* You'd introduce me to symphonies and the Mona Lisa. Expand my horizons. That it?

OLIVER. And poetry. Don't forget poetry.

IRIS. Shakespeare.

OLIVER. Emily Dickinson.

IRIS. So you'd introduce me to Shakespeare and Beethoven and that crowd. And what was I supposed to introduce *you* to?

OLIVER. Oh, I didn't think directly about that. Not straight on. I didn't paint any pictures. I just thought that I'd show you this world of higher thought and beauty and it would awaken in you this desire to –

IRIS. Jump your bones?

OLIVER. Not exactly the words I would have used then. Or now.

IRIS. What words *would* you use now?

OLIVER. *(not answering the question)* And what if I *had* asked you for a date – ? Back then.

IRIS. I probably would have been flattered. That you looked down and noticed me.

OLIVER. Oh, come on, "down." I was a geek. How can a geek look down on anyone?

IRIS. You think everybody didn't know good stuff was going to happen for you? Why do you think Ted beat you up? He was paying you back ahead of time.

OLIVER. But you would have gone out with me? If I'd asked?

IRIS. No, actually, I probably would have made some kind of crack, and then I would have told the gang, and they would have given you shit, too.

OLIVER. You would have told them?

IRIS. Yes, I would. You had too high an opinion of me. I mean, I wasn't that nice a person.

OLIVER. Oh, don't do that. I mean, kids, for Christ's sake, teenagers – they're all too concerned with not being laughed at to worry about perspective, kindness, any of that. I mean, I don't expect, much less blame – But you know this. You must have seen it in your own kid, your daughter. What's her name?

IRIS. Natalie.

OLIVER. Nice.

IRIS. You realize, she's older now than you and I were the last time we saw each other?

OLIVER. Wait a second, let me – say that again –

IRIS. You're older, no, *she's* older now than you and I were –

OLIVER. – the last time we saw each other. Right.

IRIS. It's true.

OLIVER. Senior prom was it?

IRIS. Probably.

OLIVER. You looked great that night. In case you didn't know.

IRIS. You remember vividly.

OLIVER. Kind of a dark blue dress, off the shoulders.

IRIS. *(disturbed)* Hey –

OLIVER. What's the matter?

IRIS. What are you doing?

OLIVER. Just remembering.

IRIS. Well, don't.

OLIVER. Oh?

IRIS. Let it alone.

(a beat)

OLIVER. I'm sorry.

IRIS. No, it's OK. I mean, I'm not offended.

OLIVER. No?

IRIS. But it's –

OLIVER. OK.

IRIS. We're here right now. All that other stuff –

OLIVER. No, I agree.

IRIS. Good.

OLIVER. Except that's sort of the point, isn't it? A reunion. These are the kinds of thoughts that'll come up.

IRIS. Except I chose not to go, remember? You didn't see me at the luncheon.

OLIVER. That's true.

IRIS. So it's not like that's something I'm really eager to revisit.

OLIVER. But you decided to come by here to see me in particular?

IRIS. That's different. Ted called me –

OLIVER. Called you at your job?

IRIS. We talk about you sometimes, so he knew that I'd be interested you were coming to visit.

OLIVER. You talk about me?

IRIS. I watch you on the tube, on the TV –

OLIVER. Really.

IRIS. It's not like I know dozens of people who have TV shows. And sometimes Ted and I, yes, we talk about some of what you say. Not that my opinion's worth all that much, but I like what you do. I like what you – I think you make good points.

OLIVER. It never particularly occurred to me that you'd watch the show.

IRIS. Oh sure.

OLIVER. What do you know?

IRIS. Sure.

(a beat)

OLIVER. *(very directly)* You and Ted– the two of you– you never –

IRIS. What? Did he ever get into my pants? No. Somehow I missed that treat. Why? Would it damage your opinion of me –

OLIVER. I didn't think you had.

IRIS. Is that a load off your mind?

OLIVER. I hoped you hadn't.

IRIS. You hoped – ?

OLIVER. It's something that – it's none of my business – something I couldn't help but wonder.

IRIS. When?

OLIVER. Back then, in school. And tonight.

IRIS. Wondering tonight about back then, or wondering tonight about – what – now?

OLIVER. The thought, the question occurred. Some of the looks you were giving each other –

IRIS. You're reading in.

OLIVER. It's none of my business anyway.

IRIS. Believe it or not, he's pretty nuts about Lianne and the boys. Whatever else there is about him, that part – I've never heard anything but that he walks the real straight and narrow when it comes to his family. He really is good with Lianne.

OLIVER. I'm glad to hear that. She's somebody who needs to be cared for. Looked after.

IRIS. From what you can see.

OLIVER. Which, yeah – Here I am, shooting my mouth off. Fifteen minutes and I'm – Sorry. But, you know, my heart went out to her.

IRIS. Oliver?

OLIVER. OK.

IRIS. She's not yours to rescue.

OLIVER. No, of course not.

IRIS. The hundred bucks was a nice gesture, but let it go at that.

OLIVER. No, of course. It would be presumptuous. Of course.

IRIS. And, about me and Ted – news flash: it *is* possible to be friends with a guy without making it with him.

OLIVER. I'm sure.

IRIS. Or don't you have any women friends?

OLIVER. Many.

IRIS. And do you sleep with all of them?

OLIVER. Hardly any.

(a beat)

Gee, I wonder if I've had enough to drink. What do you think?

IRIS. Loosen your leash. You're not driving.

OLIVER. Yes, true. Do you think he's going to be long? Dropping off Lianne?

IRIS. Her mama's just down the road. But, you know, there's a chance he might get stuck in one of those family things.

OLIVER. Yeah, I've heard about them.

IRIS. Family things?

OLIVER. No, I was just wondering. See, Ted gave me a lift out here –

IRIS. Oh, right.

OLIVER. Not that I haven't enjoyed myself.

IRIS. Sure, how often do you get conversation this profound in New York?

OLIVER. When I think of how afraid I used to be of him – Do you know – well, maybe I shouldn't say this –

IRIS. Say anything you feel like –

OLIVER. He said earlier, before you were here – he made this comment about how I probably haven't thought about him in years. I wasn't going to tell him, but I think about him everyday.

IRIS. Really?

OLIVER. When I was a freshman, I was standing in the boys' john, you know, at the –

IRIS. Urinal?

OLIVER. There was a whole row of these ones that go all the way down to the floor.

IRIS. OK, I get the picture.

OLIVER. So I'm standing there, and I'm –

IRIS. – yes, and?

OLIVER. – and suddenly I feel this hand in the middle of my back and a push. I step forward to catch my balance, and my foot's in the thing now, and down my right leg there's this trail.

IRIS. Ted?

OLIVER. He laughs. I go into one of the stalls and close the door and wait for it to dry. I was late to class, and I was sure everybody knew, could tell. All the times he pounded me, those I've mostly forgotten. But I go into a public john, particularly if there's a lot of noise and rowdiness – at a ball park? – I feel my back tense up –

IRIS. Waiting to be pushed again?

OLIVER. Like that's something you needed to know, right? Well, maybe this visit will turn out to be therapeutic.

IRIS. Because you've made peace with Ted, you'll stop tensing up in the men's room?

OLIVER. You know, it would be worth the whole trip.

(**IRIS** *laughs.*)

IRIS. Would you like a lift back? Where are you staying, the Taylor Arms?

OLIVER. Good guess.

IRIS. I'll take you back.

OLIVER. If it's no trouble.

IRIS. It's what I have a car for.

OLIVER. Well, great. What about Ted? He comes back, we're not here –

IRIS. We'll leave a note.

OLIVER. Right.

IRIS. Or call him when we get where we're going.

OLIVER. "When we – "?

IRIS. Or however it turns out.

OLIVER. Sure.

IRIS. Ted is not a problem in any case. You ready?

OLIVER. Let me finish my drink.

(He is sitting in his chair as he drinks. She drifts over. He puts down his glass. She swoops down and kisses him on the lips, then stands up straight again. He is a little startled, but not displeased. He looks up at her, a little bemused. Lights fade.)

Scene Two

(The living room of **IRIS**'s *home. We see the door to the front road. We also see a bit of the kitchen and a door that leads offstage to a bedroom. In half-light, under music,* **OLIVER** *and* **IRIS** *enter, a little unsteadily. They are laughing and all over each other. He tosses his jacket over a chair and turns to* **IRIS**, *who points him in the direction of the bedroom and gives him a little shove to propel him woozily offstage. She turns around to check the front door handle, making certain – as we will realize later – that it is unlocked. Then she turns, and, begins to take off her blouse as she herself enters the bedroom. The door to the bedroom is left ajar. The music fades and the lights come up a bit, indicating the passage of time. The sound from the bedroom gives evidence of hot and heavy activity. In the middle of this, the front door opens. It is* **TED** *carrying a tote bag. He gently closes the door behind him and makes his way to the bedroom door to check on their progress. He opens the tote bag and pulls out a flash camera. The sound from the bedroom begins to build in intensity.* **OLIVER** *is evidently approaching climax.* **TED** *watches for his moment, then slips through the door. A series of four or five white flashes erupt from the bedroom as well as sounds of confusion.* **TED** *now ambles out of the bedroom. He turns on the lights in the living room and sits in an easy chair where he can have a good view of the door to the bedroom. He waits. A beat or two and* **OLIVER** *enters, having hastily put on his pants and a T-shirt. He looks at* **TED**.*)*

TED. *(affably)* Got to tell you something, Oliver – got to compliment you: You looked like you knew what you were doing in there.

OLIVER. *(bemused)* You took pictures.

TED. Five of them.

OLIVER. Pretty fast shooting.

TED. *(holding up the camera)* Motor. Advances the film automatically, recharges the flash. Fast shutter, fast film – when I blow them up, won't be any doubt who it is. A side of you your TV viewers have never seen in sharp, clear shots.

OLIVER. What are you planning on doing with these sharp, clear shots?

TED. Thought I'd send them to your wife.

OLIVER. So, what you told me before wasn't strictly the truth. When you said you had no agenda.

TED. No, I had an agenda.

OLIVER. This was your agenda.

TED. This was my agenda.

OLIVER. Why you invited me over to your place, why you kept filling my glass, why Iris so conveniently appeared –

TED. Yup.

OLIVER. I didn't see it coming.

TED. You underestimated me.

OLIVER. I don't know if I'd put it that way.

TED. I really don't care *what* way you'd put it. I'm pretty fucking *tired* of you *putting* it, OK? All your opinions. And the attitude tonight like I was supposed to be grateful to you for sharing this crap. Like you were the grand high rabbi of New York granting me an audience. Like you really have something meaningful to tell me. That you even *believe* you do. That I should look to you for wisdom? What movie to see, how to be a good human being? You tell me, "Oh, I couldn't take money for saying something nice about a movie, that wouldn't be *honest.* I have *integrity.*" Well, buddy, I've got a camera full of your integrity.

OLIVER. I'm sorry if I offended you.

TED. The only thing that makes you sorry is that I'm sitting here with this. Otherwise you wouldn't give two shits about what I think. Isn't that right?

OLIVER. Actually, no, I don't think so.

TED. No, you don't think so what? You wouldn't give two shits or you would?

OLIVER. I might even give three.

TED. Well, you're gonna give more than that.

OLIVER. Or else you send these pictures –

TED. – to your wife.

OLIVER. My wife. Wow. What if I tell you that someday you'd be embarrassed that you did this? That maybe you'd dislike yourself kind of a lot?

TED. Not be able to face myself in the mirror in the morning?

OLIVER. We have to live with what we do. With the consequences.

TED. Well, the consequences here are that we'll have money we didn't have before.

OLIVER. "We?"

TED. I have a partner.

OLIVER. Of course.

TED. How do you think I got in?

OLIVER. She left the door unlocked.

TED. But, see, I know what you were doing –

OLIVER. What was I –

TED. Just now. What you were trying to do: appeal to my better nature.

OLIVER. Didn't work too well, hunh?

TED. I enjoyed watching you try. There's one thing I wish –

OLIVER. What?

TED. That you were wearing glasses. For old times' sake.

(He mimes breaking them.)

OLIVER. I could take my contacts out.

TED. Would they go crunch under my heel?

OLIVER. They're the soft kind. Probably just make a little squish.

TED. Not worth it.

OLIVER. Sorry.

TED. Oh, before I forget –

*(**TED** reaches into his pocket and pulls out the hundred dollar bill.)*

I want the stamp back.

OLIVER. Excuse me?

TED. The pink stamp. Give it to me.

OLIVER. I bought it. Your wife and I made a deal.

TED. Null and void. Here's your hundred dollars. You think I don't know what you were doing, you fuck?

OLIVER. Buying a stamp.

TED. Buying *some*thing, that's for sure. *Thinking* you were buying something. She's *my* wife. She has problems, it's *my* job. You want to play the big man, descend from a fucking cloud with alms for the poor – What gives you the right? As if we'd accept a handout from you.

OLIVER. You don't want my money.

TED. No, I don't.

OLIVER. Unless you can take it.

TED. I don't care if you get it or not.

OLIVER. No, I understand. If you accept something from me that might smell of concern, sympathy –

TED. – pity –

OLIVER. – that makes you a wuss. Blackmail, on the other hand –

TED. You *owe* this to me.

OLIVER. OK, this part I'm having trouble following. I haven't seen you in God knows how many years, how can I –

TED. Where do you put your money, Oliver?

OLIVER. Where everybody – my wallet.

TED. No, I don't mean your cash, I mean your *money*. Stocks? Mutual funds?

OLIVER. Some real estate and, yeah, mutual funds.

TED. Been pretty good for you the past few years, hunh? Mutual funds.

OLIVER. Did OK.

TED. All those companies in the portfolio, streamlining their operations. Getting rid of dead wood. Getting rid of divisions that aren't performing up to par. Closing down plants that aren't showing a good enough return.

OLIVER. Did you have any particular plant in mind?

TED. How much did your portfolio go up? How much did you make while some people filed for unemployment?

OLIVER. So this is what – reparations?

TED. Call it whatever you want to call it.

(calling)

Iris, come on out here.

(a beat)

Iris!

*(A beat. **IRIS** appears wearing a robe. She avoids looking at **OLIVER**.)*

IRIS. Something you need me for?

TED. Toss me his coat.

IRIS. You can't get it yourself?

TED. I want you to do it.

*(A beat and **IRIS** gets it, hands it to **TED**. **TED** reaches into the inside pocket, pulls out **OLIVER**'s wallet, opens it, takes out the stamp, puts the hundred back in the wallet and puts the wallet back into the pocket. Feeling around, **TED** finds **OLIVER**'s checkbook and tosses it to him.)*

This is how it's going to go: you're gonna write me a check. After I cash it, I'll send you the film.

OLIVER. A check?

TED. Fifty grand.

IRIS. Wait a minute. You said twenty. On the phone, you said –

TED. I changed my mind.

IRIS. You said twenty, we'd split twenty.

TED. So now we'll split fifty.

IRIS. That's not what we agreed.

TED. Look at him, he can afford it.

IRIS. That's not the point.

TED. You couldn't use twenty-five grand?

IRIS. I don't need that much.

TED. Fine, take what you want. More for me.

IRIS. You can't just change things –

TED. Hey, whose idea was this? Whose plan?

IRIS. Like this is so brilliant? You think this is inventing the wheel? Discovering Velcro?

TED. It's gonna solve some problems, isn't it?

OLIVER. Sorry to interrupt, but I've still got a question or two.

TED. Ask.

OLIVER. If I don't write the check –

TED. Old business. I send the pictures to –

OLIVER. – to my wife, yes. But what size were you thinking of sending?

TED. Size?

OLIVER. Of the pictures? The prints? Five by seven? Eight by ten?

TED. What does it matter?

OLIVER. Just want to have a complete grasp of the situation.

TED. Eight by ten.

OLIVER. Matte? Glossy?

TED. I like glossy. Is that enough of a grasp? You gonna write that check?

(**OLIVER** *hesitates, then writes the check, tears it off.*
TED, *to* **IRIS** –)

Bring it here.

IRIS. Ted –

TED. Do you want your share?

IRIS. I think I've done enough for my share. I think I've done *more* than enough for my share.

TED. Oh?

IRIS. You were supposed to come in sooner. You were supposed to come in before –

TED. Before he slipped it to you?

IRIS. I've done my share.

TED. *(to* **OLIVER***)* You think she's mad at me?

OLIVER. Could be.

TED. Iris, you mad at me?

IRIS. Another thing you didn't do the way we said. The way we agreed.

TED. Iris, I'm at a loss here. I'd offer you more money by way of compensation, for my bad timing when I came in, but you just said you don't want more. Of course, even if you decided to do me the favor of accepting more, we'd still have to figure out how much your compensation should be.

(**OLIVER** *gets up and hands* **TED** *the check while* **TED** *is still looking at* **IRIS**.)

OLIVER. Here.

TED. *(to* **IRIS***)* Just how much is it worth, Iris? Your what – your honor? What would be an appropriate figure? Give me an estimate in round numbers.

IRIS. Very funny, Ted.

(**TED** *laughs as* **OLIVER** *moves back across the room.* **TED** *looks at the check. His expression changes.*)

TED. What's this supposed to be?

OLIVER. My bet is glossy eight-by-tens go for fifteen bucks a pop here. Five times fifteen is seventy-five, a little extra for tax and postage and an envelope. You can mail them to her care of the address at the top of the check there. The mail will be forwarded to wherever she decides to live.

TED. Wait a second. What are you playing here?

OLIVER. She left me two weeks ago. My wife.

TED. Left you?

OLIVER. Packed up her bags and took off. It's one of the reasons I came to the reunion. Something to do with myself. She and I were supposed to go to St. Thomas this weekend. But she announced two weeks ago that she had other plans with somebody else for the rest of her life. I think she's being optimistic about the "rest of her life" bit, but the upshot is she's gone. And frankly, it wouldn't upset me all that much if she got some evidence that I'm managing OK. That I'm not lacking for company. I hope I'm smiling in at least one of those shots. But the point is you don't have a situation here with blackmail potential. The conditions don't exist.

(a beat)

TED. This is – you're just making this up, right? You're bluffing.

OLIVER. No, it's the truth. But if you don't believe me, call my bluff. *Make* the prints. Send them to her.

(He begins to laugh.)

The joke's on me, really. I wanted to believe that you'd pulled it together. I wanted to believe that you – I don't know why. Probably the sentimental streak in me. Probably the part of me that believes in midnight basketball for troubled youth and rehabilitation programs in prisons and buying UNICEF cards. But, Jesus Christ, you were a putz in high school and you're still a putz. Only difference is now you're an older putz.

(a beat)

I should probably get dressed now. Pardon me, Iris.

*(Brushing past **IRIS**, he heads for the bedroom. A beat, **TED** puts down the camera and begins to head for the bedroom.)*

IRIS. Ted, now don't –

(**TED** *pushes her aside and disappears into the bedroom. The sound of violence as* **TED** *is evidently working* **OLIVER** *over pretty badly.* **IRIS** *stands at the door.*)

Ted! Stop! Don't!

(*She heads into the bedroom but is shoved out quickly as the beating continues. She looks around the kitchen. She is about to reach for a knife, but thinks twice and grabs a heavy skillet. She goes into the bedroom and there is a sudden bonging sound. Then silence. Now* **TED**, *bleeding from the back of his head, stumbles into the living room and falls down, dazed.* **IRIS** *returns to the room, still holding the skillet.* **TED** *turns to look at her.*)

IRIS. I told you to stop.

TED. You some kind of maniac?

IRIS. You were hurting him.

TED. He laughed at me.

IRIS. Are you OK?

TED. You hit me with a fucking skillet, what do you think? Shit, I'm bleeding.

IRIS. I want you out of here. Out of my house.

TED. This is because I came in late, right? Because I let him do it to you?

IRIS. I won't be part of beating somebody up.

TED. What do you call what you just did to me? Stupid bitch.

(**OLIVER**, *sporting a bloody nose, appears in the doorway to the bedroom.*)

IRIS. *(brandishing the skillet)* You want more?

TED. *(shrinking)* All right, all right.

(**IRIS** *picks up the camera, opens it, takes the film. Closes the camera, tosses it to* **TED**.)

IRIS. Go.

TED. You realize what you're doing?

IRIS. I'm gonna miss getting your Christmas cards.

TED. You know what you're forgetting, Iris? You live here. You live here, I live here. This clown, he didn't live here even when he did. Which one of us you going to be seeing next week at the Texaco? Or if by some miracle the plant actually does open again, the line in the cafeteria? Or, you're at the bar and Stuart lets you persuade him to serve you one drink more than what you know is your limit – and what Stuart knows is your limit – and you're in no shape to get behind the wheel, which one of us you gonna turn to for a lift home? Who's gonna be there?

(TED exits. IRIS puts the skillet down. She goes to the kitchen and grabs a fistful of paper towels and hands them to OLIVER.)

OLIVER. I got drunk, I got laid and I got beaten. My homecoming is complete.

(IRIS doesn't react.)

How are you? You OK?

IRIS. I'm swell.

OLIVER. You look a little woozy.

IRIS. I'm not used to handing out concussions.

OLIVER. Maybe you ought to sit down, put your head between your legs, do some deep breathing.

IRIS. Excuse me?

OLIVER. Could do you some good. Why don't you try it?

IRIS. What the fuck's the matter with you?

OLIVER. The matter?

IRIS. Don't you understand what just happened here? Don't you get it?

OLIVER. Sure.

IRIS. I set you up. Ted and I were in this together.

OLIVER. OK.

IRIS. Do you understand that?

OLIVER. Yes.

IRIS. I was part of trying to get money out of you. I got naked and got into bed with you, I let you put yourself inside me so that he could take pictures so that we could get money out of you.

OLIVER. No, I figured that much out.

IRIS. It's called blackmail. Extortion. It's a crime. You were going to be the victim of a crime. You *are* the victim of a crime!

OLIVER. No, really, you don't have to shout.

IRIS. So what is this attitude about? This concern shit?

OLIVER. Well, I figure you must have had your reasons for doing what you did.

IRIS. My reasons are I wanted money.

OLIVER. Because you needed it.

IRIS. Of course I needed it. You think I would have done this for pleasure?

OLIVER. Well, a guy could hope.

IRIS. That was the point. You showed up. You didn't bring your wife –

OLIVER. Ted smelled an opportunity, he called you –

IRIS. And I did it. I actually did it. Dumb.

OLIVER. Well, not *that* dumb. Four or five weeks ago, it would have worked. No question. You just had the bad luck of depending on my wife to play the wifely part the way she was supposed to. Believe me, I share in your disappointment. No, four or five weeks ago, I would have written the check.

IRIS. But four or five weeks ago, if you still thought your marriage was solid, would you have hopped in the sack with me?

OLIVER. Hmmm.

IRIS. Probably not.

OLIVER. Well, the impulse would have been there. The impulse has always been there. I think I'm paying you a compliment. If you consider it a compliment. Anyway, that's not what we're talking about.

IRIS. What do you think we're talking about?

OLIVER. Why you agreed to do this thing with Ted you wouldn't have done otherwise. You're not somebody who would do something like this if you weren't desperate. You want to tell me about it?

IRIS. No.

OLIVER. If you need money so bad –

IRIS. Who doesn't need money?

OLIVER. Well, actually, I don't. Not at the moment. But you told Ted before you only wanted to take what you needed.

IRIS. So?

OLIVER. So it sounded like there was a specific sum you had in mind. A specific sum, which suggests a specific something you need it for.

IRIS. Everybody has their problems. Nothing unusual. No big deal.

OLIVER. Something to do with your daughter? With Natalie? Or her kid?

(a beat)

IRIS. Actually, yes, she needs open-heart surgery. My granddaughter.

OLIVER. Really?

IRIS. No!!! Jesus Christ, I could tell you *any*thing! How do you stay alive?

OLIVER. I just want to understand. You did this thing. This thing you wouldn't do unless you were desperate. But you see I understand cuz I'm going through my own stuff. You're desperate, I'm not in the greatest place in the world –

IRIS. You miss your wife.

(This hits home. A beat.)

OLIVER. You know what, maybe this was supposed to happen. No, no, hear me out –

IRIS. This was supposed to happen? You were supposed to get blackmailed and beaten?

OLIVER. Well, not that exactly, but here we are –

IRIS. Give me a break –

OLIVER. You and me. Maybe there's some good that's supposed to come out of this.

IRIS. What is this "supposed to?" If something was "supposed to," then that means that someone had to do the supposing. Who? Some higher power? Do you think this is part of some higher power – some *plan* – *God?* You think that God put you in my bed and had Ted work you over so that we were *supposed to* find each other? For what?

OLIVER. Comfort? Consolation?

IRIS. You know, right now I almost want to beat you up myself. Where do you get this shit?

OLIVER. I'm sorry.

IRIS. What, now you're gonna apologize to *me?*

OLIVER. What do you want me to do? Tell me what you want me to do. Do you want me to yell at you? Call you names? Would that make you feel better?

IRIS. Then you might be recognizably human. You should be furious. Right now, if you were a human being, you'd want to run Ted over with a truck and –

OLIVER. – and do something to you? What? Beat you up? Slap you around?

IRIS. I'm not saying I want you to do that. But at least it's something I'd understand.

OLIVER. OK, what don't you understand?

IRIS. Is it a Jewish thing? This thing you're doing?

(**OLIVER** *looks at her for a second, then begins to laugh. She looks at him sternly for a second, then she begins to laugh, too. They laugh long and hard. Finally, they subside.*)

IRIS. How's your nose?

OLIVER. Fine.

IRIS. You going to do anything about Ted?

OLIVER. Like maybe press charges? No.

IRIS. Any particular reason?

OLIVER. It would mean sticking around this town some more. That's not something I'm real eager to do.

(a beat)

What do you say you come back with me?

IRIS. Come back with you?

OLIVER. To New York. I'm serious.

IRIS. Oliver, I don't have any stamps to sell you.

OLIVER. Do you have somebody right now?

IRIS. None of your business.

OLIVER. You don't. You don't, I don't. It could work.

IRIS. Sure.

OLIVER. Why not? Why not? If we decide we want it to? What's to keep it? If we just decide. If we just decide this is what we want to do. This is what we want to be. That it's our choice how our lives turn out. Think about it.

IRIS. We would last maybe three weeks.

OLIVER. OK, fine, I'll settle for that.

(As she stands, he takes hold of her arm. Pressing his head against her stomach, he begins to cry. She hesitates, then she puts her arms around him. The grief pours out of him.)

IRIS. OK now. OK.

(She holds him as the lights fade.)

AUTHOR'S NOTES

This play is loosely based on something that a friend told me happened to him.

He did indeed return to the town where he'd lived during his high school years for a reunion. He was indeed approached by the bully who had given him grief. They started drinking together, and my friend awoke to find himself in bed with a naked woman and a camera pointed their way by the bully in a blackmail frame-of-mind. Newly separated from his wife, my friend made the mistake of laughing and telling the bully why he wasn't inclined to pay up, and the bully indeed responded by beating the hell out of him.

After commiserating, I asked my friend if he minded if I tried to write something based on his experience someday. He graciously gave me permission. More than twenty-five years later, I finally figured out how to tell it. (I hasten to add that Oliver is not a portrait of my friend.)

I decided to make the woman an active conspirator rather than an anonymous hooker and to give the bully a wife he loves. And to place the incident into a larger context.

At the time I was writing this, the *New York Times* was running a series called "The Downsizing of America." Much of it was about the closing of plants in the midwest and what this did to the towns in which they were located. These articles and other personal input from people I knew in the area fed the development of the script.

The play premiered in 1998. I suppose it would be a simple matter to update it, but I prefer to keep it set in the period that informed the play's writing. Reading it with today's eyes, the script seems to have anticipated the open culture war between the capitals on the coasts and the towns between that came to be much discussed later. (When I wrote this script, the terms "red states" and "blue states" weren't in popular use.) Rather than drag the story into the present, I think it's worth allowing the piece to suggest some of the roots of the battles that followed (and, as I write these notes, are still raging).

When the show received its New York premiere in 2009 (with its 1998 setting intact), it did so when recent economic events couldn't help but add other resonances to the play. The action is set at a time when a lot of people who had expected to spend their whole working lives in American industry saw decisions and policies originating in New York and Washington prompt their employers to export their jobs to the third world. In 2009, more decisions and policies from New York and Washington were driving large numbers of middle-class workers to the unemployment lines. Some of the people who had profited (through their stock investments) from the downsizing of the blue collar workers were now seeing their paper profits evaporate and their own lifestyles threatened by the same forces they used to tacitly endorse. As I write this, the movie-reviewing show Gene Siskel and Roger Ebert were broadcasting from Chicago when *Flyovers* is set (and to which the text refers) has just been canceled. My hunch is that today Oliver, like Ted, would be looking for work.

So much for why I keep the play in 1998.

About the characters:

Oliver thinks of himself as a reasonable and good guy. He is unaware of the degree to which he appears condescending. (After all, he is putting so much effort into *not* appearing condescending.) He is surprised by how gratified he is by Ted's seeming overtures of friendship. And, shaken by the breakup of his marriage, he is vulnerable to Iris's advances. The personal upheaval he's recently experienced has to be bubbling underneath resulting in the occasional reaction unconnected to what's immediately at hand.

Ted should not be played as an overt bully. If the actor will simply pursue the objectives of appearing to be an ingratiating host and trying to win Oliver's respect for his ideas, then the rest will fall into place. The menace does not have to be underlined. Also, Ted's objective in the scene with Lianne is to protect her from embarrassing herself. He loves her, and her distress pains him. (Incidentally, I would like to say thanks here to William Petersen, the original Ted, who suggested I write Ted's exit speech in scene two. This illustrates the benefit of developing material with a very smart actor.)

Lianne should not be played for craziness but rather for the effort she puts into *not* looking out of control, though whenever she feels her mask slipping her instinct is to shift into an apologetic mode.

Iris may be the play's most complicated character. She is no angel. She agreed to the plan with Ted and, despite misgivings, she goes ahead. (Part of the fun of playing her should be charting when she is on the verge of deciding not to go through with it and why she ultimately chooses to stifle her instincts and do it anyway.) There is a line she won't cross, though, and in the second scene she is a little surprised to discover it. Not prone to self-pity, she has little patience with the feeling of victimization that runs as an undercurrent in much of Ted's material. Within these parameters, there is a fair amount of room. Amy Morton played her as a functioning alcoholic with a fatalistic streak. Michele Pawk played her as a good-time gal working at not looking too closely at the darkness. Both performances were brilliant.

Incidentally, the title of the play came from a story I heard about a network executive talking to a producer who had pitched him an ambitious TV project. "They'll get it in New York and they'll get it in Los Angeles," the executive was supposed to have said, "but will the flyovers get it?" (Friends living in the Midwest tell me that the term has some currency there.)

I do a fair amount of traveling, and I've noticed that the resentment of New York and L.A. is almost palpable. This has been the subtext of a startling number of conversations I've had with people around the country – this anger on the part of many that so much of the culture is dictated to them by people on the coasts who are blithely indifferent to what's going on elsewhere. This often is expressed in comments like, "Well, maybe being from New York this won't look like much to you, but we like it." Ted may be Oliver's bully. New York and L.A. are widely perceived to be the twin bullies of the United States.

This isn't restricted to cultural concerns, of course. In an era in which, despite decisions which have brought the US economy to the brink, corporate executives still reap millions putting into place plans that translate into the decline of whole towns, it's easy to see why those newly unemployed might be pissed at the urban centers where most of these corporate executives live and work. Though I disagree with Ted's methods and his bigotry, I can't help but think he has reason to be angry.

-Jeffrey Sweet

ACKNOWLEDGEMENTS

Thanks to the various actors, writers, directors and friends who helped me find my way on this one, among them – Polly Adams, Lindsay Crouse, Kit Flanagan, Peter Frechette, Tim Halligan, John Christopher Jones, K.C. Landis, Melissa Manchester, Kristine Niven, Jeff Perry, John Rothman, James Sherman, Marc Vann and the members of Ensemble Studio Theatre. Special thanks to the folks at Naked Angels for a particularly valuable workshop: Jace Alexander, Nicole Burdette, Jodie Markell and Geoffrey Nauffts.

**Also by
Jeffrey Sweet...**

After the Fact

Bluff

Porch

I Sent a Letter to my Love

Please visit our website **samuelfrench.com** for complete descriptions and licensing information

OTHER TITLES AVAILABLE FROM SAMUEL FRENCH

AFTER THE FACT

Jeffrey Sweet

Dramatic Comedy / 1m, 1f / Simple Set

An old man confronts a young reporter over the errors she has made in his best friend's obituary.

"Gave me a special nudge…and I am tempted to elbow all my peers…[Sweet has] talent and a facility for the small sounds of life, simple communications that often barely conceal major attitudes
and emotions."
– *Chicago Sun Times*

SAMUELFRENCH.COM

OTHER TITLES AVAILABLE FROM SAMUEL FRENCH

BLUFF

Jeffrey Sweet

Dark Comedy / 3m, 3f / Simple Set

Emily and Neal are doing fine as a new couple in New York until her brash and vulgar stepfather comes to town for a convention. Gene brings with him all of the contradictions Emily has been trying to bury. Incorporating theatrical techniques pioneered by Chicago's Second City comedy troupe, *Bluff* alternates between farce and drama to build a disturbing comedy about love and family on a collision course.

This provocative play, a hit when Jon Cryer starred in it at the Tony Award winning Victory Gardens Theatre, was nominated for the Joseph Jefferson Award for Best New Work.

"A new American play I simply cannot get out of my mind. Gene and his…view of frayed family ties haunt the memory. *Bluff*…leaves a very big impression. I want to see it again."
— *Chicago Tribune*

"The real hook is that the actors play with the audience members' heads, breaking the fourth wall at unexpected moments, and sometimes even breaking the fifth wall, speaking as themselves rather than their characters. It's actually quite funny. Mr. Sweet is…surprisingly successful at mixing comedy and drama."
— *The New York Times*

"For a play with an essentially despairing view of love in an age of no-fault divorce and casual hook-ups, *Bluff* often has a teasing, frothy feel. That's partly due to Sweet's cunning ear for dialogue; he has a knack for burying stinging repartee under rambling tangents…The aforementioned theatrical shuffling burnishes the 80-minute play's glow of delight."
— *Newsday*

SAMUELFRENCH.COM

OTHER TITLES AVAILABLE FROM SAMUEL FRENCH

PORCH

Jeffrey Sweet

Drama / 2m, 1f / Simple Set

Best Drama Award of 1978: Society of Midland Authors.

A woman, her father and an old boyfriend confront each other on a Midwestern front porch.

"A family play about open warfare and buried love between a father and daughter written with subtlety and increasingly compelling emotion."
– *The New York Times*

"It's lovely to watch this finely wrought, gracefully executed play draw an audience completely into its world."
– *The Chicago Tribune*

SAMUELFRENCH.COM

OTHER TITLES AVAILABLE FROM SAMUEL FRENCH

I SENT A LETTER TO MY LOVE

Book and Lyrics by Jeffrey Sweet,
Music by Melissa Manchester

2m, 3f / Various sets

This soul stirring journey of renewal begins on a Maine summer night in 1955. Gwen appears to rent a cottage from Amy and her wheelchair bound brother Stan. She is venturing into a new life following the death of her mother, whom she nursed. On a whim, Amy places a "Wanted to Correspond" ad, but her notions of romance backfire when only Stan responds. Just when things get out of hand, longing, love and loyalty conspire to open new doors for all in this seamless blend of well developed characters and memorable songs by the noted pop artist.

"An inspiring fable ... [with] a richly romantic score."
— *The New York Times*

"Possesses a charm and literacy and attention to character all too rare in modern musicals.... Manchester's aching melodies, tinged with autumnal fire, are matched by rich, poetic lyrics."
— *Chicago Sun Times*

"Moving and tuneful.... An altogether delightful charmer."
— *New York Post*

"Almost 'Letter' perfect."
— *North Shore Sunday.*

"Engrossing 'Letter' delivers."
— *Boston Globe*

SAMUELFRENCH.COM

www.ingramcontent.com/pod-product-compliance
Lightning Source LLC
Chambersburg PA
CBHW070648300426
44111CB00013B/2317